Contents

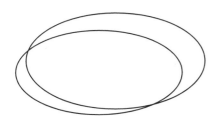

Dear Teachers and Parents,

The preschool years are an important time for children to learn and to practice skills needed to make and to keep friends. Research has shown that the single best childhood predictor of good mental health, achievement, and other positive adult development is not school grades or classroom behavior but rather the child's ability to get along with peers and to develop quality relationships. Friendships provide children the opportunity to successfully build a bridge to the world beyond themselves while at the same time enhancing their emotional and cognitive development.

My Friends is divided into three sections. The first section, **Our Friends,** gives center activities related to the friendship theme. It contains suggestions and directions for your classroom in the following areas:

Room Decor:

Creating a visual environment gives children the opportunity to instantly identify the unit's theme. It also helps to stimulate positive thoughts of making learning fun as soon as the children walk into the room. An inspiring room decor opens their imagination to all the possibilities available to them as they continue learning.

Story Time and Reading Center:

Blessed is he who reads this book (Revelation 22:7). Opening a child's mind to reading sets a foundation for learning that is unmatched. Opening a child's mind to the Bible builds a foundation for eternity. A suggested list of books is offered in this section to share and to make available for the children's exploration. Use these brightly illustrated children's books as a stepping stone for other activities and projects. *(Please note that some of the books are out of print, but may still be available through the Internet, at libraries, or in personal collections.)*

Places to Go and People to See:

This section helps make the unit real by offering a "real life" approach to the lessons. You will find suggestions for field trips and guest speakers related to the theme.

Language and Alphabet Skills:

A thematic approach to language and the alphabet provides a great way to remember the basics. This section offers suggestions for activities, games, and ideas for stretching these basic skills.

Music! Music! Music!:

Speak to one another with psalms, hymns, and spiritual songs. Sing and make music in your heart to the Lord (Ephesians 5:19). Music makes a heart joyful and enriches the learning opportunities for children. Learning thematic songs adds an additional dimension to each lesson.

Movement:

Movement offers suggestions for active ways to experience the lesson through exercise and games. It also provides an opportunity to stretch, wiggle, and laugh. Movement encourages fun and thematic ideas for a break in the day.

Imaginative Play:

Themed props and playthings that further enhance and encourage playing are suggested in this section. This offers children the opportunity to pretend to "be" and to experience part of the theme.

Home Living Center:

Here you will find suggestions for thematic additions to your year-round home living center. Role playing becomes real as the children use actual items found in their homes. Creating a warm and fun "home environment" encourages the imagination to soar.

One Stop Thematic Units

My Friends

Celebrating God's Love Together

Deborah Saathoff and Jane Jarrell

Illustrator
Dan Farris

SAINT LOUIS

Scripture quotations taken from the HOLY BIBLE, NEW INTERNATIONAL VERSION®. NIV®. Copyright © 1973, 1978, 1984 by International Bible Society. Used by permission of Zondervan Publishing House. All rights reserved.

Text Copyright © 2001 Deborah Saathoff and Jane Jarrell
Illustrations copyright © 2001 Concordia Publishing House

Published by Concordia Publishing House
3558 S. Jefferson Avenue, St. Louis, MO 63118-3968

Manufactured in the United States of America

Teachers who purchase this product may reproduce pages for use in the classroom and to send home for parents to use with children.

All rights reserved. Except as noted above, no part of this publication may be reproduced, stored in a retrieval system, or transmitted, in any form or by any means, electronic, mechanical, photocopying, recording, or otherwise, without the prior written permission of Concordia Publishing House.

1   2   3   4   5   6   7   8   9   10   10   09   08   07   06   05   04   03   02   01

Blocks Center:

Building with blocks opens the mind to all sorts of possibilities. Themes can be expanded in this area by adding simple, little toys to use with the blocks.

Sensory Table:

Experiencing different textures and shapes is a great way to learn. The sensory table that you fill with sand, water, or other materials to encourage and to build the exploration of the sense of touch can also be tailored to build on the theme. Included in this section are some suggestions for ways to do that.

Science:

Learning how things work and why they work is just the beginning of discovering God's majesty. Some simple experiments and explorations related to the theme are found in this section.

Math:

Number recognition, one-to-one correspondence, counting, patterns, and shapes make up a young child's math curriculum. You will find thematic suggestions for these kinds of activities in this section.

Arts and Crafts:

Included are instructions for theme-related projects. Children's art is a colorful expression of themselves. It is the thrill of starting with nothing and ending with something. It offers a method for teaching all sorts of important skills and the children enjoy it.

Snack Time:

This section offers recipes and suggestions for treats that build on the theme. They are fun to make, fun to eat, and fun to share. Snacks that match the theme add spice to the day. *(Please note that the ingredient lists only tell you the items needed. Please adjust amounts according to your class size.)*

The second section of *My Friends* is **Friendship Toolbox**. Here you will find specific suggestions for developing the emotional and affective skills needed to get along well with others. While not designed to be presented in a center format, the material here provides activities that can be used not only with the center theme presented in **Our Friends**, but throughout the year in any theme you may study.

A deep and personal connection with the Savior is the single most important relationship we can nurture in children. Activities and suggestions for nurturing this relationship are given in **Our Friend Jesus**. Again, these will complement the **Friendship** centers for a thematic study but are not limited to them.

Faith Foundations are found at the end of each section. One way to make God's love appear real to a young child is through discussions about tangible things. Each Faith Foundation highlights special friendships found in the Bible and will offer suggestions for applying Scripture to the lesson, plus activities and questions to help further discussion. Ultimately, Faith Foundations becomes the foundation for all other ideas in hopes of pointing little ones to Christ. By no means is this considered the only place to build the faith of children in your care. Simply pointing out to two friends working cooperatively in the blocks center, "I like the way you are working so nicely together. Isn't it wonderful that God gives us friends?" is an example of one way to integrate God and His love for us into every activity.

Use these ideas as printed, adapt them, pick and choose, or modify them to fit your needs. We hope this will be both a resource and a springboard of ideas that will be a blessing to you and your children.

Deb and Jane

Our Friends

What is a friend? A friend is someone who makes you feel special. He might laugh at your jokes or enjoy the same kind of books, toys, or games. Friends care about each other and treat one another with kindness and respect. This special relationship is called "friendship." Something important to remember about friendship is that having a good friend means being a good friend. Found in Matthew 7:12, the Golden Rule says it this way: *Do to others what you would have them to do to you.* God gave us a great blessing in our friends, so let's celebrate the gift of friendship.

Room Decor

✔ Design and prepare a friendship quilt as detailed in the Arts and Crafts section.

✔ Have the children work cooperatively with friends to create extra long paper chains to drape around the room.

✔ Decorate a chain of paper dolls to look like classroom friends. (See pattern on page 7.)

✔ Make and display the friendship trees described in Arts and Crafts section.

✔ Display the "I Like You Because ..." posters from the Alphabet and Language Skills activity.

Story Time and Reading Center

*Aldridge, Josephine Haskell. *The Best of Friends*
Aliki. *We Are Best Friends*
Capucilli, Alyssa Satin. *Biscuit Finds a Friend*
Carle, Eric. *Do You Want to Be My Friend?*
Carle, Eric. *The Very Lonely Firefly*
Cohen, Miriam. *Will I Have a Friend?*
Hallinan, P.K. *A Rainbow of Friends*
Henkes, Kevin. *Chester's Way*
Henkes, Kevin. *Jessica*
Hoban, Russell. *Best Friends for Frances*
Hobbie, Hollie. *Toot and Puddle: A Present for Toot*
Hobbie, Hollie. *Toot and Puddle: You Are My Sunshine*
*Hopkins, Lee Bennett. *Best Friends* (Poems)
*Hutchins, Pat. *Titch and Daisy*

Katz, Bobbi. *Could We Be Friends?: Poems for Pals*
Lewis, Kim. *My Friend Harry*
Lobel, Arnold. *Frog and Toad Are Friends*
*Martin, David. *Lizzie and Her Friend*
Mavor, Sally. *You and Me: Poems of Friendship*
Mayer, Mercer. *A Boy, a Dog, a Frog and a Friend*
Monson, A.M. *Wanted: Best Friend*
*Ness, Caroline. *Let's Be Friends*
Sathre, Vivian. *Three Kind Mice*
Silverstein, Shel. *The Giving Tree*
*Stevenson, James. *Fast Friends: Two Stories*
Wallace, John. *Little Bean's Friend*

This book is out of print, but may be available through the Internet, at libraries, or in personal collections.

Bible Story Books

Bleat!: The Parable of the Lost Sheep (CPH, Phonetic Bible Stories)

Blessings: Jesus Blesses the Children (CPH, Phonetic Bible Stories)

Choose!: Ruth (CPH, Phonetic Bible Stories)

Come to Jesus: Jesus Blesses the Children (CPH, Hear Me Read Book)

David and Jonathan (CPH, Arch Book)

The Day the Little Children Came (CPH, Arch Book)

Down through the Roof (CPH, Arch Book)

The Good Samaritan (CPH, Arch Book)

He Remembered to Say Thank You (CPH, Arch Book)

Jesus Blesses the Children (CPH, Arch Book)

Jesus Forgives Peter (CPH, Arch Book)

Jesus the Good Shepherd (CPH, Arch Book)

Joseph Forgives His Brothers (CPH, Arch Book)

The Kind Samaritan (CPH, Arch Book)

Mary and Martha's Dinner Guest (CPH, Arch Book)

Sit Down: Mary and Martha (CPH, Hear Me Read Book)

The Tan Man: The Good Samaritan (CPH, Phonetic Bible Stories)

Thank You, Jesus: Jesus Heals 10 Men with Leprosy (CPH, Hear Me Read Book)

Through the Roof: Jesus Heals a Paralyzed Man (CPH, Hear Me Read Book)

Too Tall, Too Small: Zacchaeus (CPH, Hear Me Read Book)

Who Will Help?: The Good Samaritan (CPH, Hear Me Read Book)

Zacchaeus (CPH, Arch Book)

Alphabet and Language Skills

Friendship Writing Center

You Will Need:

Assorted sizes and colors of paper
Unlined index cards
Construction paper in various colors
Envelopes of various sizes
Stamps and ink pads
Stickers
Markers and/or crayons

How to Do:

1. Provide a writing center to make greeting cards to send to friends.
2. You may want to make "mailboxes" for the students so the greetings can be mailed.

Some ideas for the mailboxes are:

✗ Create a simple pocket chart with each child's name and picture on a pocket to use as the mail center.
✗ Place a line of white lunch-size paper bags along a wall or bulletin board. Put each child's name and picture on or over the bag, or you may choose to have the children decorate their own mailboxes for your mail center.

My Friends' Name Notebook

You Will Need:

Photocopied pictures of each child
Poster board or other stiff paper (8 ½" x 11")
Three-ring binder or brass fasteners
Glue
Markers, pencils, or crayons
Three-ring protector pages (or laminating materials)
Tape
Tracing paper (or see-through typing paper)

How to Do:

1. Glue each child's picture onto one of the poster board pages.
2. Write the child's name on the page with his or her photograph.
3. Slide each page into a three-ring protector page (or laminate).
4. Place the pages into a three-ring binder or punch holes and use the brass fasteners to make a book.
5. Provide tape, tracing paper, crayons, markers, or pencils.
6. Let the children tape the tracing paper over a friend's name and trace the letters.

Poster/Bulletin Board Matching Game

You Will Need:

A photo of each child
Each child's name tag strip
Plastic letters of the alphabet in a basket

How to Do:

1. Place all the pictures of the class on a table next to all of the name tags of the children.
2. Let the children match the names to the pictures.
3. Next, let them match the plastic letters in the alphabet basket to each name.
4. Attach magnets to name tags and photos. Use them along with the plastic letters on a surface where they stick (i.e., filing cabinet, white board, etc.)

What's My Letter?

You Will Need:

Alphabet floor puzzle or large cut out letters of the alphabet
Name tags

How to Do:

1. Have the children form a circle on the floor. Place all of the letters of the alphabet in the center of the circle.
2. Give each child a name tag with his or her name written on it.
3. Go around the circle and have the group say each child's name and take turns finding the letter of the alphabet that is at the beginning of each child's first name.

My Friends' Favorite Things Book

You Will Need:

Camera and film
Small photo album
Stickers

How to Do:

1. Take photos of the children doing their favorite activities. Have duplicate copies developed.
2. Make labels listing the children's names in each picture.
3. Create a "My Friends' Favorite Things" book by sliding the photos into the albums and labeling them.

(Use for page 1.)

My friend, my friend, who do you see?

(Use for child's photo.)

I see

looking at me.

who do you see?

"My Friend, My Friend" Book

You Will Need:

A copy of *Brown Bear, Brown Bear, What Do You See?* by Eric Carle
A photocopied picture of each child
8 ½" x 11" white paper
Patterns (see pages 10 and 11)
Three-hole protector pages (or laminating materials)
A three-ring binder

How to Do:

1. Duplicate the photo frame pattern on page 10 so each child has a page for his or her photo. Make one copy of the introductory page on page 10.
2. Read Eric Carle's *Brown Bear, Brown Bear, What Do You See?* to the class.
3. Glue each child's photo into a frame.
4. Write each child's name in the appropriate blanks on the next page provided.
5. Insert the pages into three-hole protector pages or laminate them.
6. Beginning with the introductory page, place the pages in order in a three-ring binder.
7. Read the book to the class.

* Place this book in the language arts center for students to "read."

Friend Find

You Will Need:

Pocket chart with 26 pockets (this can
   be made from felt or poster board)
Cut out uppercase letters
Glue
Scissors
Index cards with the lowercase letters
   written on them (laminated, if possible)

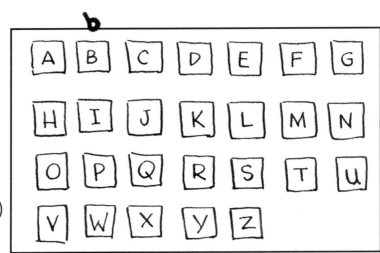

How to Do:

1. Glue an uppercase letter to the front of each pocket.
2. Have the children match the lowercase letters by placing
    them into the pocket of their uppercase match or "friend."

I Like You Because ... Poster

You Will Need:

12" x 12" white construction paper
A photograph of each child
Glue
Markers

How to Do:

1. Glue each child's photograph to a piece of paper. Write that child's name on the paper.
2. Ask the other children to tell one thing they like about the child. Write their responses on the
    personalized page. Complete a page for each child.
3. Arrange the pages to form a poster or banner in the classroom.
4. Read each child's poster out loud as it is placed on the wall. Leave them up for several weeks.

* This could also be done daily or weekly as "student of the day/week" activity. The comments could then be done at this time rather
than all at the same time.

Friend Match

You Will Need:

Friends patterns (see pages 13, 14 and 15)
Markers

How to Do:

1. Duplicate the patterns of children on pages 13, 14, and 15. Make sure you have 52 children.
2. Write the uppercase letters on 26 of the children. On the remaining 26, write the lowercase letters.
3. Laminate for durability.
4. Let the children match "friends" by matching the uppercase and lowercase letters.

Uppercase/Lowercase Match

You Will Need:

Uppercase and lowercase alphabet letters

How to Do:

1. Give each child the uppercase letter that is at the beginning of his or her first name.
2. Place all of the lowercase letters on the floor.
3. Have the children take turns finding the lowercase letter that matches the upper-case letter that begins their first name.
4. Once this has been done successfully, switch the letters and start all over.

Buddy Brag Bag

You Will Need:

An old lunch box, drawstring bag or canvas tote bag.
Favorite items from home

How to Do:

1. Give each child a turn to take the "Buddy Brag Bag" home to collect some of his favorite things.
2. When the child brings the bag back to class, have him tell about the special things brought and why they are special to him.

* This could also be done in connection with the "Student of a Week" display, or as a replacement for "Show and Tell."

15

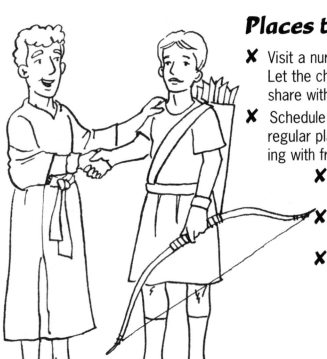

Places to Go and People to See

✘ Visit a nursing home or an assisted living facility in your community. Let the children bring special crafts or samples of their work to share with the residents.

✘ Schedule a visit to a favorite playground or simply emphasize before regular playground time that playgrounds can be places to enjoy playing with friends.

✘ Visit a hospital to sing or to bring something special to share with the patients.

✘ Invite your pastor to speak to the class about Jesus as Savior and Friend.

✘ Invite people to dress as biblical characters who were friends (i.e., David and Jonathan, Paul and Barnabas, Peter and John, etc.) and speak to the children.

Music! Music! Music!

✔ "Be Kind to Your Web-Footed Friends"
✔ "Puff the Magic Dragon"
✔ "Getting to Know You" (from the musical "The King and I")
✔ "Won't You Be My Neighbor?" (Mr. Rogers's theme song)
✔ "I Can Be Your Friend" (from the Veggie Tales video "Are You My Neighbor?")

Do You Know This Friend of Mine?
Melody: "Do You Know the Muffin Man?"

As students and teacher sit together, call one child forward to stand next to the teacher while everyone sings:

Do you know this friend of mine,
Friend of mine, friend of mine?
Do you know this friend of mine
Who's come to school today?

Have everyone call out the child's name. Let that child pick the next child to be featured. Keep singing until everyone has had a turn.

Share Your Toys
Melody: "Row, Row, Row Your Boat"

Share, share, share your toys.
Share them with your friends.
It's so kind to share your toys.
Share and be a friend.
Let's all share our toys.
Share with all our friends.
It's so kind to share our toys.
Sharing with our friends.

If You're Friendly and You Know It
Melody: "If You're Happy and You Know It"

If you're friendly and you know it,
Clap your hands (clap, clap).
If you're friendly and you know it,
Clap your hands (clap, clap).
If you're friendly and you know it,
Then your face should surely show it.
If you're friendly and you know it,
Clap your hands (clap, clap).

The More We Get Together
Melody: "Did You Ever See a Lassie"

The more we get together, together, together,
The more we get together, the happier we'll be.
For your friends are my friends,
And my friends are your friends.
The more we get together, the happier we'll be.

Second stanza: The more we play together ...
Third stanza: The more we work together ...

Two Fat Gentlemen (Finger Play)
(Hold hands in two fists, fingers facing your body, thumbs up.)

Two fat gentlemen
Met in a glen.
Bowed most politely, (Bend one thumb.)
Bowed once again. (Bend the other thumb.)
How do you do? How do you do? (Bend both thumbs with each "How do you do?".)
And how do you do again? (Bend both thumbs.)

Repeat using:
Index fingers: "two thin ladies"
Ring fingers: "two happy children"

Middle fingers: "two tall policemen"
Pinkies: "two little babies"

17

Where Is Thumbkin? (Finger Play)

(Begin with both hands behind your back.)

Where is Thumbkin?

Where is Thumbkin?

(Bring one fist around with the thumb pointing up.)

Here I am!

(Bring the other fist around with its thumb pointing up and facing the other thumb.)

Here I am!

(Bend one thumb.)

How are you today sir?

(Bend the other thumb.)

Very well I thank you.

(Put one fist behind your back.)

Run away.

(Put the other fist behind your back)

Run away.

(Repeat with the rest of the fingers: Pointer, Tall Man, Ring Man, and Pinkie. Can also be sung to the melody for "Frere Jacques.")

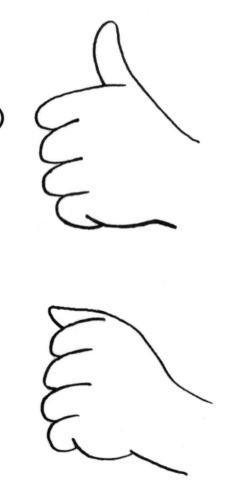

Movement

✔ Play *"Let's Find a Friend"* by having all the children sit in a circle. Select one child by drawing a name from a container. Have that child stand in the middle of the circle. To the melody for "The Farmer in the Dell," have everyone sing:

(Kathryn) finds a friend,
(Kathryn) finds a friend,
Heigh, ho, the derry-o,
(Kathryn) finds a friend.

The first child chosen then chooses another from the circle. They hold hands and walk around inside the circle while everyone sings. The next verse begins with the second child choosing a friend to join the group in the center and holding hands with the first two. Everyone sings:

(Sarah) finds a friend,
(Sarah) finds a friend,
Heigh, ho, the derry-o
(Sarah) finds a friend.

Continue until all children have been chosen and are now holding hands inside what had been the original circle. Everyone sings:

We all found a friend,
We all found a friend,
Heigh ho the derry-o,
We all found a friend

✔ Play *"Row, Row, Row, Your Friend!"* by placing an area rug or blanket on the floor to be the "boat." Two friends sit facing each other with legs out, knees slightly bent, and feet touching.

Have the partners hold hands and "row" by moving back and forth in a push-me, pull-you rhythm as they sing "Row, Row, Row Your Boat."

✔ Play *"Follow the Friend."* This is a new name for an old favorite— "Follow the Leader."

✔ *"Will You Be a Friend of Mine?"* Let each child be the "leader" and call out the action to be done as the children sing the last line of the following stanza sung to the melody for "Mary Had a Little Lamb."

Will you be a friend of mine,

Friend of mine, friend of mine?

Will you be a friend of mine?

And (choose an action) around with me?

(Leader could choose to jump, hop, crawl, dance, walk, run, spin, etc. according to your space.)

✔ Play *"Call and Catch."* You will need a balloon (not helium-filled). Have the children form a circle. Choose one child to begin the game in the center of the circle. This child holds the balloon and calls out a friend's name as he throws the balloon up high.

The child whose name was called runs into the circle and tries to catch the balloon before it touches the ground. That child then becomes the caller for the next round. (A more competitive version requires the child to catch the balloon in order to become the caller. If the balloon is not caught, the child in the middle continues until the balloon is caught.)

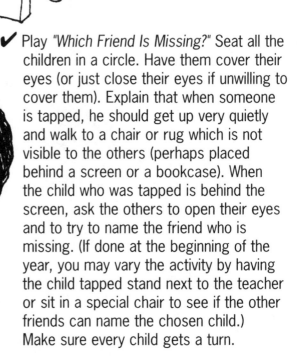

✔ Play *"Which Friend Is Missing?"* Seat all the children in a circle. Have them cover their eyes (or just close their eyes if unwilling to cover them). Explain that when someone is tapped, he should get up very quietly and walk to a chair or rug which is not visible to the others (perhaps placed behind a screen or a bookcase). When the child who was tapped is behind the screen, ask the others to open their eyes and to try to name the friend who is missing. (If done at the beginning of the year, you may vary the activity by having the child tapped stand next to the teacher or sit in a special chair to see if the other friends can name the chosen child.) Make sure every child gets a turn.

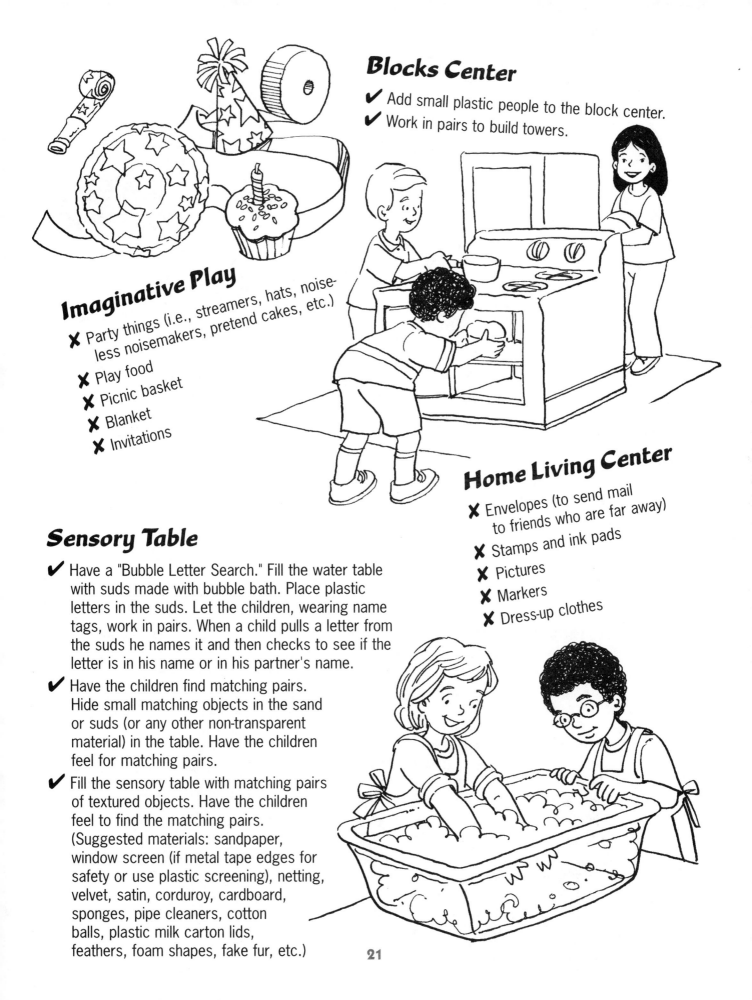

Blocks Center

✔ Add small plastic people to the block center.
✔ Work in pairs to build towers.

Imaginative Play

✗ Party things (i.e., streamers, hats, noise-less noisemakers, pretend cakes, etc.)
✗ Play food
✗ Picnic basket
✗ Blanket
✗ Invitations

Home Living Center

✗ Envelopes (to send mail to friends who are far away)
✗ Stamps and ink pads
✗ Pictures
✗ Markers
✗ Dress-up clothes

Sensory Table

✔ Have a "Bubble Letter Search." Fill the water table with suds made with bubble bath. Place plastic letters in the suds. Let the children, wearing name tags, work in pairs. When a child pulls a letter from the suds he names it and then checks to see if the letter is in his name or in his partner's name.

✔ Have the children find matching pairs. Hide small matching objects in the sand or suds (or any other non-transparent material) in the table. Have the children feel for matching pairs.

✔ Fill the sensory table with matching pairs of textured objects. Have the children feel to find the matching pairs. (Suggested materials: sandpaper, window screen (if metal tape edges for safety or use plastic screening), netting, velvet, satin, corduroy, cardboard, sponges, pipe cleaners, cotton balls, plastic milk carton lids, feathers, foam shapes, fake fur, etc.)

21

Science

Talk to a Friend

You Will Need:

Nail (and a hammer if you are using tin cans)
Two empty yogurt cups (or tin cans)
Scissors
String (about 15′ long)
Bar of soap
Paper clips

How to Do:

1. Use the nail to poke a hole in the center of the bottom of each yogurt cup.
   (If using tin cans, have an adult make a hole with a hammer and nail.)
2. Wet the bar of soap. Rub one end of the string on the soap, then roll the
   tip of string between your fingers to form a point.
3. Poke the pointed end of the string through the hole in the bottom of the cup.
4. Reach inside the cup with your fingers and pull the string a few inches.
   Tie the end of the string to a paper clip.
5. Repeat steps 2–4 with the other end of the string and the second yogurt cup.
6. One friend holds one of the yogurt cups while the other friend walks across
   the room with the other cup until the string is pulled taut.
7. Have one friend speak into her cup while the other friend holds his cup to his ear.
   Ask: **Can you hear what your friend is saying?**
   * Variation: Each friend holds her yogurt cup to her ear. When the string between
   them is pulled tightly, pluck the string like a guitar string. Ask: **What do you hear?**
   Provide a simple explanation for the ability to hear the sounds by having them
   notice how the string moves when it is plucked. Tell them that voices can also
   make the string move because sound moves the air.

Magnetic Bottles

You Will Need:

4 clean, dry, clear plastic soda or water bottles *with* caps
4 large magnets
4 lengths of yarn about 15" long
Assorted small metal and non-metal objects
Magnetic bingo chips (located in party supplies at some discount
   department stores and often packaged with a magnetic wand)
Magnetic numbers and/or letters
Heavy scissors or razor knife (for adult use only)
Hot glue gun (for adult use only)
Bright plastic tape
Water
Salt

How to Do:

1. Glue the caps onto each of the bottles.
2. Cut the tops off of each of the bottles so that objects
   can be placed inside.
3. Place various small metal and non-metal objects into the first bottle.
4. Tape the top of the bottle back into place.
5. Place the magnetic bingo chips into the second bottle and fill with water.
6. Tape the top of that bottle back into place.
7. Put the magnetic numbers and/or letters into the third bottle.
8. Tape the top back into place.
9. Place small magnetic objects into the last bottle. Fill with salt.
10. Tape the top back into place.
11. Attach a magnet to each bottle using the lengths of yarn.
12. Let the children experiment by holding the magnets to the
    sides of each bottle to see what comes to the magnets.
13. The children may record their observations by drawing the
    objects, letters, or numbers attracted or by counting the
    number of bingo chips drawn to that bottle's magnet.

Magnets (Friends Like to Be Together)

Combine the study of magnets with a discussion of reasons children like to be with friends. (Possible answers: they like many of the same things; they like the way the other person treats them; they have fun doing many of the same things together.)

Pulling Power Magnet Center

You Will Need:

A strong magnet
A piece of paper
A piece of cloth
A piece of aluminum foil
A paper clip

How to Do:

1. Let a child try to pick up the paper clip with the magnet.
2. Cover the paper clip with a piece of paper. Let another child try to pick it up with the magnet.
3. Repeat using the cloth and the foil.

Friends in Nature

✔ Observe an ant farm and watch the ants work together.

✔ Place a bird feeder outside near a classroom window. Observe the birds that come to eat.

✔ Make bird feeders.

— Smear a pinecone with peanut butter, roll it in birdseed, and suspend it from a tree branch using yarn or twine.

— Hummingbird feeders can be made using a small, clear, plastic container filled with one part sugar dissolved in three parts hot water with beet juice added (hummingbirds are attracted to red). Suspend from a tree branch with string.

✔ Make a birdbath.

You Will Need:

1 plastic gallon milk jug
Scissors (for adult use only)
Trash can lid or shallow plastic bowl
Sand or brick
Small rocks

How to Do:

1. Slice off the top of the plastic milk jug to form a base for the birdbath. (Birds prefer baths that are elevated.)
2. Cut curves in the top to accommodate an upside-down garbage can lid or shallow plastic bowl.
3. Put sand or a brick in the milk jug to keep it from tipping over.
4. Place the trash can lid or the shallow plastic bowl on the milk jug, topside down.
5. Fill the lid or bowl with a layer of small rocks.
6. Fill the lid or bowl with water.
7. Place the birdbath in a place set back from sidewalks or traffic areas.

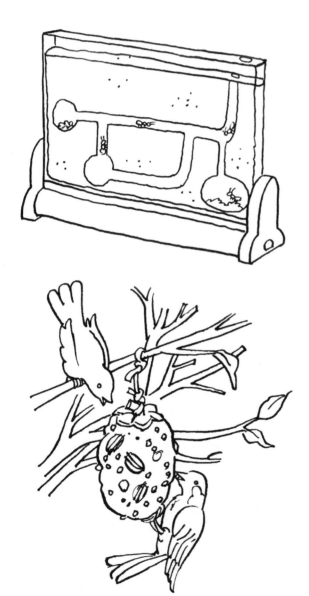

✔ If children have access to a creek, stream, or pond, make an underwater viewer.

You Will Need:

A half-gallon milk carton
Clear plastic wrap
Snug-fitting rubber band or tape

How to Do:

1. Cut off both the bottom and the top of the milk carton.
2. Stretch the plastic wrap over the bottom, securing it with the rubber band or tape.
3. Lower the viewer into the water and look through the open end of the carton.

✔ Host a "Be a Friend to Nature" day and have children and their families help pick up litter in a play area nearby. Be sure to require or provide gloves for the workers!

✔ Watch a caterpillar metamorphose into a butterfly. Then set the butterfly free. (The "Butterfly Garden" by Insect Lore contains instructions, a feeding kit, an enclosed clear plastic observation area, a coupon to redeem for caterpillars, and additional information. It can be purchased for about $20 at toy, novelty, nature, or educational supply stores, or through the Internet at www.sciencestuff.com or HYPERLINK http://www.liveandlearn.com.)

✔ Have a classroom pet.

✔ Take a nature walk and count all the animals (nature friends) you see.

✔ Plant a *"Friendship Flower."*

You Will Need:

1 carnation for every two children
Scissors or knife (adult use only)
1 small plastic cup per student
Assorted food colorings

How to Do:

1. Use the scissors or knife to split each flower stem in half.
2. Assign each child a partner.
3. Give each pair one flower.
4. Ask each child to select a food coloring color. Have an adult pour the coloring into the cup. (Make sure each child has a different color than his partner.)
5. Ask each child to place his side of the flower stem into the food coloring.
6. Set aside. Watch what happens. (This is a good introduction to the way plants get food and drink.)

Math

✘ Cut the tops off of one-pint milk cartons or use juice cans. Label each of the cartons or cans with a number. Make wooden stick people by gluing cutout pictures of children from magazines or catalogs to construction paper and laminating and attaching to wooden craft sticks. Have the children place the correct number of friends into each labeled container.

✘ Have several different "Help Me Meet My Friend" mazes for the children to complete. (See pages 27–29 for reproducible mazes.)

✘ Do "Find My Friend" matching pages. (See pages 30–31 for reproducible pages.)

FINISH

START

✘ Different and Alike (Venn Diagrams)

You Will Need:

Laminated copies of the two large overlapping circles pattern provided on the next page
Pictures of different toys, foods, activities, objects, etc., cut from magazines and
    catalogs, glued to construction paper, and laminated to make them more durable
Laminating materials

How to Do:

1. Have the children work with a partner.
2. Place one friend's name by one circle and the other friend's name by the other.
3. Have each child place pictures of things he likes in his own space. Things both friends like should
   go in the portion that overlaps.
   * If left unlaminated, each pair could cut and glue their choices directly onto the paper.

✘ Have the students sort and match pairs of socks or mittens that have been separated in a basket.

✘ To reinforce one-to-one correspondence, duplicate the pattern of a child on page 34 so that you
have 20 children. On 10 of them write the numerals 1 through 10. On the remaining 10, place
stars, dots, or other small markings to correspond with each number. Let the children match the
"friends." (You can expand or reduce the number to accommodate the children's age and skill.)

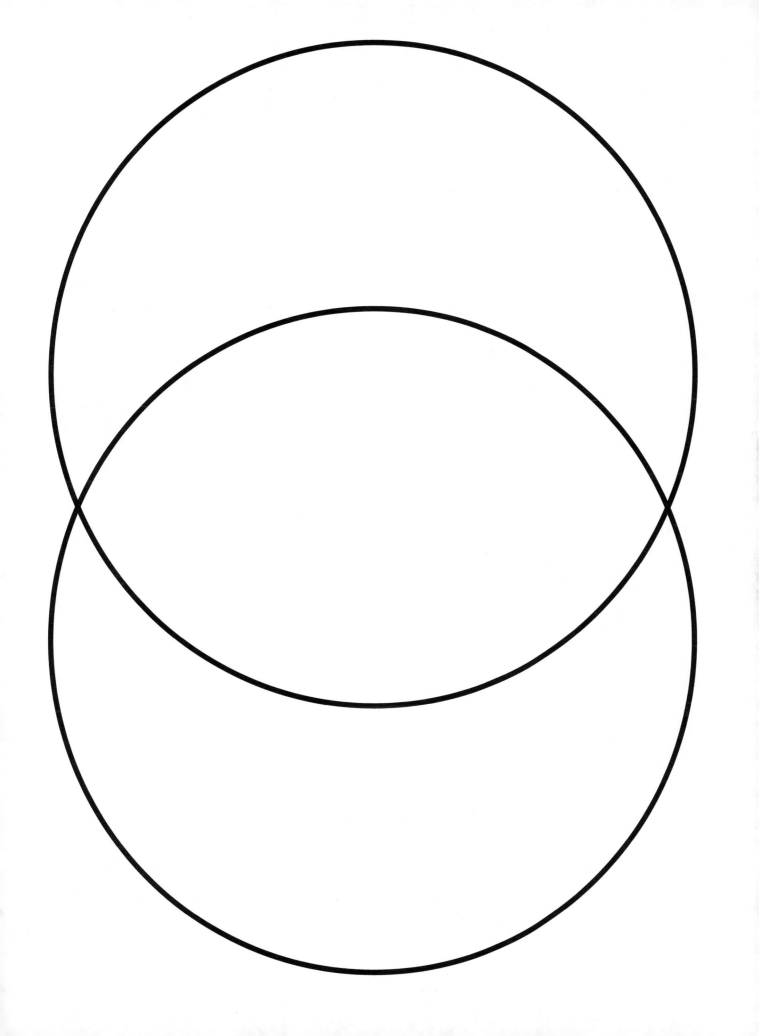

34

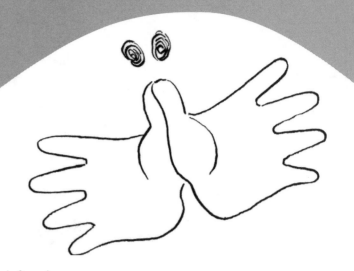

Butterfly Buddies

You Will Need:

Washable tempera paints
Brush
Large pieces of construction paper
Crayons or markers
Tub of warm water
Paper towels
Paint smock or old shirt for each child

How to Do:

1. Assign each child a partner or "buddy."
2. Paint one child's right palm and the other child's left palm.
3. Have each child press her hand onto the paper so that the thumb becomes the butterfly's body and the palm and fingers are the wings. (Make sure the thumbs overlap.)
4. Have each child make two thumbprints at the top for antennae.
5. Add color to the antennae with crayon or marker.
6. Have each child wash his hands in the tub of water before leaving the area and dry with a paper towel.

Cooperation Collages

You Will Need:

Circle stickers in several colors
Magazines and/or catalogs
Scissors
Glue or glue sticks
Large sheets of construction or butcher paper

How to Do:

1. Determine how many groups you want. Choose one color of circle stickers for each group.
2. Place a circle sticker on the back of each child's hand.
3. Announce that children with the same color sticker will be working and cooperating together.
4. Have each group create a collage of items by cutting pictures of things from the magazines and catalogs that match their group's color.

Just My Size

You Will Need:

A large roll of butcher paper
Crayons or markers
Yarn
Glue
Scissors

How to Do:

1. Provide each child a section of butcher paper long enough for him to lie down on.
2. Assign each child a partner.
3. Let each child take a turn lying down on his piece of butcher paper while his partner traces around the body.
4. Have them switch papers and ask each child to color the person-shape to look like their partner. (Be sure to talk about hair color, eye color, clothing styles, and colors.)
5. Label each picture (e.g., Sarah by Kathyrn) and affix to a bulletin board or a classroom wall.

Friendship Collage

You Will Need:

Sheets of poster board
White craft glue
Scissors
Feathers
Ribbons
Craft sticks
Pipe cleaners
Stickers
Confetti

How to Do:

1. Have the children pair off and work together to make a collage on their poster board.
2. Write the names of the children on the poster board they decorated together.
3. Display on the classroom or hall walls.

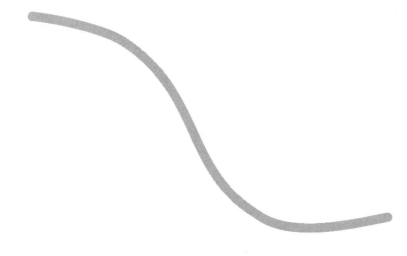

Growing Friendships

You Will Need:

Brown paper grocery sacks
Various shades of green construction paper
Scissors
White craft glue
Photograph of child
Markers
Glitter
Stickers

How to Do:

1. Crumple and twist several brown grocery sacks to form the shape of a tree trunk. Crumple and twist several other bags to form the branches. Affix them to a bulletin board, wall, or door of the classroom.
2. Help the children cut out various leaf shapes using the green construction paper.
3. Glue a photograph of each child onto the leaves.
4. Ask each child for a thought on friendship and write that on her leaf.
5. Staple the leaves to the tree.

Helping Hands Friendship Wreath

You Will Need:

Green paper or fabric (felt works well)
Scissors
Fabric paint
Ribbons
Buttons
Sequins
Beads

How to Do:

1. Have each child trace his hand onto the green fabric.
2. Cut out the hand shapes (may need adult help to cut fabric).
3. Have each child sign his hand and decorate it with ribbons and other decorative items.
4. Arrange the handprints in a circular shape to create a friendship wreath. Display the wreath on the wall or bulletin board.
   * You can also cut a piece of fabric or paper into a large circle and glue or staple the handprints onto the circle.
   * A special time to do this using green felt displayed on red felt material is during the season of Advent. Fabric Advent candles added to the center of the wreath can be "lit" each week of Advent. This makes a wonderful banner to display in the classroom, hall, or even in the sanctuary.

Friendship Quilt

You Will Need:

9" x 9" construction
 paper in various colors
White craft glue
Feathers
Buttons
Glitter
Sequins
Beads
Pictures
Scissors

How to Do:

1. Give each child a square of construction paper.
2. Set out the art supplies on a table and ask each child to decorate her piece of construction paper.
3. Make sure each child's name is visible on the decorated "quilt" square.
4. Hang the squares in a quilt pattern on your bulletin board.

Friendship Bracelets

You Will Need:

Pony beads
Alphabet beads
Thin elastic
Scissors

How to Do:

1. Have the children string the beads onto the thin elastic making sure to get the name strung on the bracelet too.
2. Cut the elastic the desired length and tie in a knot to keep the beads on the bracelet.
3. Make another bracelet to share with a friend.

The Friendship Tree

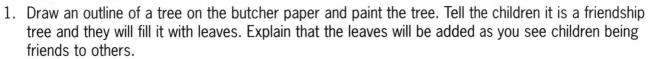

You Will Need:

Butcher paper, at least 5' long
Paint
Scissors
Green construction paper cut into leaf shapes
Red construction paper cut into apple shapes
  (enough for one apple per child)
Photos of each child's face
Glue

How to Do:

1. Draw an outline of a tree on the butcher paper and paint the tree. Tell the children it is a friendship tree and they will fill it with leaves. Explain that the leaves will be added as you see children being friends to others.
2. Glue each child's photo (cut to fit the apple shape with only faces visible) to an apple. Place all the apples on the tree.
3. Have an adult cut out leaf shapes to be kept in an envelope near the tree so they are always available.
4. When you observe a child being a friend to someone else, write the child's name, what that child did to demonstrate friendship, and the date on a leaf.
5. Give the leaf to that child to add to the tree. (These are very special so give only a few each day.)

"I Love You" with All My Hearts

You Will Need:

Various heart-shaped cutouts
Construction paper
Various pictures of favorite things
Glue
Sequins
Feathers

How to Do:

1. Give each child a piece of construction paper.
2. Have the children fold the paper in half lengthwise.
3. Using the various hearts and other decorating items, have the children decorate the front side of the construction paper card.
4. Allow the front of the card to dry. When dry, have the children open their cards and glue some pictures of their favorite things inside. Allow to dry.
5. Write the child's dictated message inside the card, and have that child give the card to a friend.

Fingerprint Friends

You Will Need:

Construction paper
Paint smocks
Various colors of tempera paint
Small bowls or margarine tubs
Markers

How to Do:

1. Pour paint into small containers.
2. Give each child a piece of construction paper.
3. Have the children stick their thumbs in the paint and make prints on the construction paper.
4. When the thumbprints are dry, use markers to make faces on each print to resemble friends. (Remember that God created everyone with a unique thumbprint, just like each person we know and meet.)
   * If desired, the children can use markers or crayons to add bodies to the thumbprint faces.

Helping Hands

You Will Need:

White cotton gardening gloves
Fabric glue
Paint smocks
Beads
Lace
Sequins
Fabric paints

How to Do:

1. Give each child a pair of gloves.
2. Using fabric glue, have each child decorate the gloves with beads, buttons, sequins, and fabric paints.
3. Talk about the many ways we can use our hands to serve God and others. When dry, let the children wear their "helping hands" and discuss and demonstrate ways they can use their hands to help others as they share the love of Jesus.
* The decorated gloves can also be displayed on a bulletin board with the title, "God Gives Us Helping Hands."

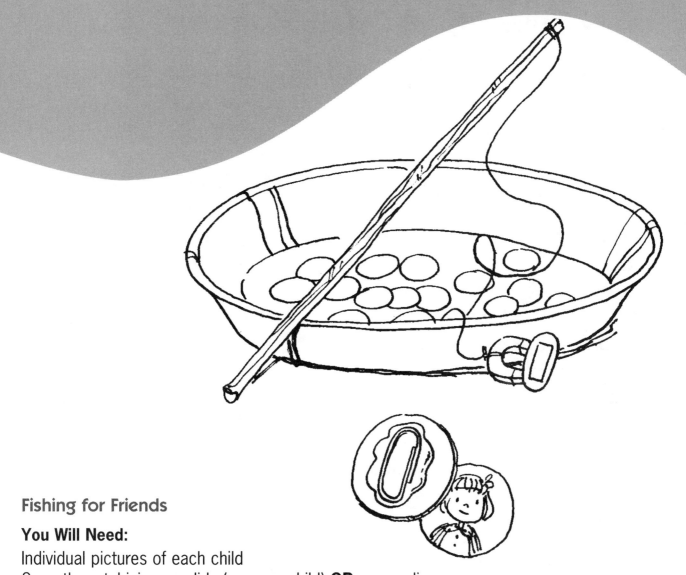

Fishing for Friends

You Will Need:

Individual pictures of each child

Smooth metal juice can lids (one per child) **OR** paper clips

Fishing poles (May be created using wooden dowels or the cardboard tubes from dry-cleaner pants hangers. Add string or twine.)

Magnets (one for each fishing pole)

A large plastic container or a small wading pool

How to Do:

1. Glue one child's picture onto each of the juice can lids. (Or glue a photocopied picture of each child onto a construction paper circle, laminate, and then attach a paper clip to each circle.)
2. Attach a magnet to the end of the string on each fishing pole.
3. Place the can lids with the children's pictures in the container or wading pool.
4. Let the children take turns "fishing for friends" by dangling the fishing pole over the lids.
5. When a picture is chosen, have the child name the friend "caught" and say something kind and complimentary about that friend.
6. The friend who was "caught" is the next to fish for a friend.

The Name Game

You Will Need:

Alphabet cookie cutters
Knife
Cutting board
Sugar shaker
Waxed paper
Tie boxes
Ribbon

Ingredients:

Prepared pound cake
Powdered sugar
Sprinkles

How to Do:

1. Cut ¾″ thick slices of the pound cake and lay out on waxed paper.
2. Ask each child to cut out a friend's name or initials from the pound cake.
3. Decorate the letters with powdered sugar and colorful sprinkles.

Spud Buddies

You Will Need:

Potato scrubber
Fork
Oven or microwave
Knife
Cutting board
Small bowls

Ingredients:

Baking potatoes
Various vegetables (peppers, carrots, zucchini, radishes, parsley, olives, etc.)
Canned cheese spread
Optional: butter, sour cream, chives, bacon pieces

How to Do:

1. Before class, scrub the potatoes and prick each with a fork three or four times.
2. Place potatoes on an oven rack and bake at 400° for about 1 ½ hours or use a microwave (cooking time varies).
3. Cut the various vegetables into different shapes and place into separate bowls.
4. Give each child a cooled potato to decorate. Have them use the canned cheese spread as the glue and the vegetables as the various facial features. If you like, photograph the group with their "Spud Buddies."

Yummy Chummy Cakes

You Will Need:
Heart-shaped cookie cutters
Waxed paper
Paper plates
Cutting board
Knife

Ingredients:
Prepared pound cake
Prepared frosting
Colorful candies

How to Do:
1. Cut thick slices of the pound cake.
2. Lay the individual slices of cake on the waxed paper. Using a heart-shaped cookie cutter have the children cut out a heart shape.
3. Place each heart-shaped cake on a plate and let each child decorate one with the icing and candies.

Gingerbread Friends

You Will Need:
Microwavable bowl
Waxed paper
Assorted candies

Ingredients:
1 package Pepperidge Farm gingerbread men
1 small package milk chocolate chips
Microwavable bowl
Small bowls
Assorted chocolate and colorful sprinkles,
   mini chocolate candies
Microwave
Spoons to stir

How to Do:
1. Place the chocolate chips into a microwavable bowl and melt them in the microwave.
2. Pour the assorted candies into the small bowls.
3. Dip the bottom half of the gingerbread men into the melted chocolate.
4. Dip the chocolate-covered gingerbread men into the sprinkles or chocolate candies.
5. Place on the waxed paper to dry.

"You're a Great Catch" Nibbles

You Will Need:

2 medium microwavable bowls
Measuring cup
Measuring spoons
Spoon
Microwave
Waxed paper
Netting
Red and white construction paper
Marker
Ribbon

Ingredients:

Larger fish-shaped crackers
2 cups white chocolate morsels
Red food coloring
2 tablespoons cream

How to Do:

1. Divide the fish-shaped crackers into two equal groups.
2. Place one cup of the white morsels into each of two separate microwavable bowls.
3. Microwave at 40-second intervals on medium power, stirring between intervals.
4. Add enough red food coloring to one bowl to make the white chocolate red. Leave the other bowl plain.
5. Allow the chocolate to cool about 3 minutes and then dip one group of the fish crackers into the colored chocolate and the other group into the plain chocolate. Lay out on the waxed paper to dry.
6. Cut an 8″ square from the netting and place ½ cup of the dipped and dried crackers into the middle of the netting, gather up the ends, and tie with a bow.

* Optional: Cut out heart shapes from the construction paper and have the children write, "You're a Good Catch" on them. Attach them to the package with a ribbon.

Friendship Face Fruit Pizzas

You Will Need:
Waxed paper
Rolling pin
Large cookie sheets
Oven
Rubber spatula
Knife and spoon

Ingredients:
Prepared sugar cookie dough
Powdered sugar
Strawberry glaze
Favorite chopped fruits
Cooking spray

How to Do:

1. Place the prepared cookie dough on a piece of waxed paper that has been sprinkled with powdered sugar.
2. Divide the dough and roll into large circles, each about 6″ in diameter.
3. Using the leftover dough, form small circles to make ears. Place the ears on the side edges of the larger circles.
4. Carefully place the cookie dough on cookie sheets that have been sprayed with cooking spray.
5. Bake in a 350° oven for 10 minutes or until lightly browned. Cool.
6. Working with partners, have the children spread the cookies with strawberry glaze and design the top of their "pizza" to resemble a face using their favorite chopped fruits.
7. Let them enjoy their pizzas with their partner.

Breakfast Buddies

You Will Need:
Small paper plates
Knives

Ingredients:
Rice cakes
Peanut butter
Marshmallow cream
Raisins
Cherries
Chocolate chips

How to Do:

1. Give each child a rice cake on a small paper plate.
2. Help them spread a layer of peanut butter on their rice cake.
3. Then spread a layer of marshmallow cream over the peanut butter.
4. Let the children choose raisins, cherries, and chocolate chips to make a friendly face.

Power Popcorn (Friends working as a team)

You Will Need:

Large bowl
Measuring cups
Measuring spoons
Small saucepan
  OR small microwavable bowl
Stove or microwave
Large stirring spoon

Ingredients:

6 cups popped popcorn
¾ cup sunflower seeds, shelled
¾ cup currants
½ cup gold raisins
½ cup peanut butter
1 tablespoon butter

How to Do:

1. Place the prepared popcorn into a large bowl.
2. Add the sunflower seeds, golden raisins, and currants to the popcorn. Mix well.
3. Melt the peanut butter and butter in small saucepan over medium heat on the stove or in a microwavable bowl in the microwave.
4. Pour over the popcorn mixture and stir thoroughly to combine all ingredients.

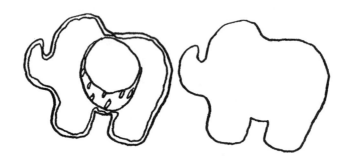

Animal Friend Sandwiches

You Will Need:

Measuring cups
Sharp knife (for adult use only)
Cutting board
Spreading knives

Ingredients:

Animal crackers, paired
¼ cup strawberry cream cheese
¼ cup strawberries

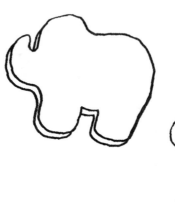

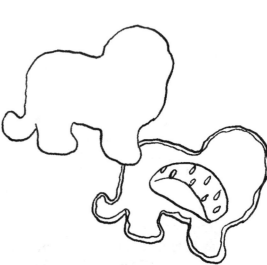

How to Do:

1. Before class, wash the strawberries and remove the tops. Slice thinly.
2. Let the children spread the flat side of each animal cracker in their pair with the flavored cream cheese.
3. Top one layer of cream cheese with a strawberry slice, then add the second animal cracker on top.

David's Friend

Scripture

And Jonathan made a covenant with David because he loved him as himself (1 Samuel 18:3).

Read *David and Jonathan* (CPH, Arch Book) or tell the story: **David and Jonathan were very close friends, almost like brothers. Jonathan gave David the robe he was wearing and his military clothes. He gave him his sword, his bow and his belt. David was going into battle and Jonathan was doing everything he could to help him get ready.**

King Saul was very jealous of David because he was afraid that David would try to take over his kingdom. When King Saul tried to hurt David, his friend Jonathan protected him.

Questions

Q God made you and He made your friends. Friends are nice to each other. How are you nice to your friends?

Q What does it mean to make a promise to your friend?

Q How do you share with your friend?

Q How can you serve Jesus by helping your friends? Do you remember to pray for your friends when they need help?

Activities

1. Make an "I Promise" chart. Write the days of the week across the top of the page. Write three important promises down the side of the page. Each day you keep that promise put a star by the promise you kept.
2. Collect clothes for children in need. Talk about the importance of helping others when they need your help. Be sure to inform the parents of this activity so they may help their child select the clothing.
3. How can you show your special friend that you love them? Make a list of ways to show the love of Jesus to others.

I Promise

	MON	TUES	WEDS	THUR	FRI	SAT	SUN
COLLECT CLOTHING		☆					
HELP OTHERS		☆	☆				
SHOW OTHERS LOVE	☆	☆	☆				

Friendship Toolbox

Young children benefit from direct instruction and guidance in skills that help them learn to get along well with others and to form and maintain friendships. On the following pages, you will find activities specifically geared to helping children develop an awareness of emotions (theirs as well as others), behaviors that demonstrate a spirit of cooperation, peaceful conflict resolution, and effective communication skills.

These activities complement the thematic unit and activities found in *My Friends*, but they may also be used on an ongoing basis throughout the year. The more these types of activities are repeated, the more quickly children will master these very important friendship skills.

Cooperation—Working with Friends

Working with others requires that children learn to exercise skills such as negotiation, cooperation, and communication. Occasionally pair children with partners to work in a center or complete a task or a project.

Pairs of Friends

Some ways to pair children together:

✗ Provide a basket with different pairs of socks or mittens that have been separated from mates. (If you'd rather not use real socks you can cut sock or mitten shapes from different colors of construction paper.) Let each child select a sock or mitten and then find the child with the sock or mitten that matches.

✗ Glue a magazine picture onto a piece of construction paper. Laminate if needed. Cut the picture into two pieces. Mix the picture pieces. Give each child one piece of a picture. Have the child find the person holding the other half of the same picture.

✗ Cut simple shapes into distinct two-piece puzzles. Have each child try to find the person holding the piece that completes his shape.

✗ Place pairs of matching stickers on construction paper shapes or index cards. Each child should find the person with the sticker that matches the one on her card.

2-4-6-8—
We Can All Cooperate!

Provide opportunities for children to work together on specific tasks or projects to help strengthen cooperative behavior.

Buddy Pictures

Set up easels with paper and paints or markers. Let children work with a partner to create pictures.

Cooperation Puzzles

Set age-appropriate puzzles out on a table to be worked on by at least two friends at a time.

Pattern Pals

You Will Need:

Unifix cubes, pattern blocks, or craft sticks that have been painted different colors

How to Do:

1. Assign children to work in groups of two or three.
2. One child creates a pattern.
3. The second child duplicates the pattern.
4. If you have three to a group, the third child checks to see if the patterns match.
5. Rotate roles so that everyone has a turn to do each task.

Emotions

Children need to learn to express their emotions in an acceptable way in order to get along with others. The first step to this is an awareness of emotions in general as well as an ability to identify one's own emotions and recognize those emotions in others.

Name That Emotion!

You Will Need:

Copies of patterns of emotions provided on this page and/or pictures of people from magazines or newspapers showing definite expressions of emotion (such as happy, sad, surprised, scared, angry, or tired, etc.)
Large index cards or pieces of poster board
Laminating materials

How to Do:

1. Before class, cut each picture so that it is separate from the others.
2. Glue each picture onto an index card or a piece of poster board. Laminate if possible.
3. Hold up the pictures and ask the children to identify the emotion. Talk about what might make someone feel that emotion.

Mirror, Mirror

Working in groups of two, have one of the partners display an emotion without using words—by using facial expressions and body language only.

You may want to introduce this activity by calling out an emotion: happy, angry, sad, sleepy, scared, surprised, etc.

See if the partner can mirror it back and, when not being directed, see if he can identify the partner's emotion. Take turns.

How Are You Feeling?

Keep the cards you made for "Name That Emotion!" handy or duplicate the pages and create a poster to display at child's-eye level. Let a child point to the picture that best illustrates the way he feels at that time.

Feeling the Same

Glue several different pictures of people displaying emotion onto index cards or other stiff paper. Ask the children to group all the people with similar emotions together: all the happy people, all the sad people, all the tired people, etc.

Paper Plate Faces

You Will Need:

Paper plates
Yarn of different colors
Scissors
Paper scraps
Glue
Googly eyes
Markers or crayons

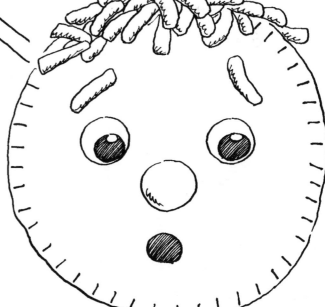

How to Do:

1. Give each child a plate to decorate to show a specific emotion.
2. Let the children share their creations and talk about the emotion depicted.
3. Each child should expand it into a story. Ask: **"Why does the face feel this way?"**

Angry Feelings

In your anger do not sin: Do not let the sun go down while you are still angry, and do not give the devil a foothold (Ephesians 4:26-27).

Get rid of all bitterness, rage and anger, brawling and slander, along with every form of malice (Ephesians 4:31).

Punching Pillow

Sew or locate a large pillow to be specially designated as the "Punching Pillow." Explain that when children get angry and feel like they need to hit something, they may hit the pillow—but *never* a friend. (You may also choose to have a "Cuddle Pillow" for holding when sad or unhappy.)

Count to Ten

Give the children alternatives to hitting, yelling, name calling, or other inappropriate expressions of anger. Here is a rhyme and a suggested activity to help little ones learn to manage their anger:

When angry feelings start to mount,

That's when I take some time to count:

One, Two, Three, Four, Five.

Counting helps me settle down.

Counting helps me fade my frown:

Six, Seven, Eight, Nine, Ten.

Manners

The Golden Rule:

Do to others what you would have them do to you (Matthew 7:12).

Manners are simply a way we get along with one another as God's children. Point out examples that small children can understand:

✔ We don't take toys away from friends who are already playing with them.

✔ We wait in line for our turn at the water fountain.

✔ We don't hit someone when we feel angry.

✔ We say "please" and "thank you."

Explain that using good manners is one way to share the love of Jesus with others.

When the children are in the centers, point out and compliment examples and make suggestions of opportunities to use good manners:

✔ Saying "please" and "thank you" when asking and receiving.

✔ Inviting someone else to join them in an activity.

✔ Saying "excuse me" and "I'm sorry" when accidents occur that hurt someone.

At snack time or in the Home Living Center, discuss and practice good table manners: Practice thanking God for the food.

✔ Wait for friends to receive food before beginning to eat.

✔ Remember to say "please" when asking for something and "thank you" after it's given.

✔ If you don't like something or don't want something, simply say, "No, thank you."

✔ Don't speak with food in your mouth.

✔ Sit nicely at the table.

✔ Wait to be excused before leaving the table.

Listening

Group the children in pairs. Have each child learn one, two, or three things about his or her partner. (Children may find out if the child has a pet; if he has any brothers or sisters; his favorite color; his favorite book; his favorite center in the classroom; etc.)

After a reasonable amount of time, have each child introduce his or her partner and tell the things they learned from the "interview."

Classroom Rules

Discuss the various rules for the classroom. Make sure the children understand why the rules are necessary. Ask: **"How do they help us obey the Golden Rule?"**

God's Rules—
The Ten Commandments
(Deuteronomy 5:6–21)

God did something marvelous for us when He sent Jesus to be our Savior. Out of gratitude for the gift of His grace to us, we gladly follow the Ten Commandments that show us how we are to behave toward Him and toward each other.

1. *You shall have no other gods.*
* Love, trust, and obey God more than anyone or anything else.

2. *You shall not misuse the name of the Lord your God.*
* Do not use God's name the wrong way; instead speak His name with respect; pray, praise, and give thanks.

3. *Remember the Sabbath day by keeping it holy.*
* Set aside special days to worship God.

4. *Honor your father and your mother.*

   * Honor, serve, love, and obey your parents.

5. *You shall not murder.*

   * Don't hurt other people with your words or actions.

6. *You shall not commit adultery.*

   * Husbands and wives are to love and honor each other.

7. *You shall not steal.*

   * Don't take what isn't yours.

8. *You shall not give false testimony against your neighbor.*

   * Tell the truth and do not speak lies about others.

9. *You shall not covet your neighbor's house.*

   * Do not wish that the things that belong to someone else were yours instead.

10. *You shall not covet your neighbor's wife, or his manservant or maidservant, or anything that belongs to your neighbor.*

   * Do not wish that the people who are faithful to others would be faithful to you instead.

(Note: Some may use alternate numbering for the Ten Commandments. These have been adapted from *Luther's Small Catechism*, CPH, 1986.)

Faith Foundations

Scripture

[Paul said:] Greet Priscilla and Aquila, my fellow workers in Christ Jesus.
They risked their lives for me. Not only I but all the churches of the Gentiles are grateful to them.
(Romans 16: 3–4)

Read the story of Paul and his friends, Priscilla and Aquila, from a children's Bible or tell the story: **Paul was a missionary who traveled around telling people about Jesus and His saving love. He would speak to people in the streets, he would visit them in their homes, and he started new churches with the help of friends.**

Priscilla and Aquila were very good helpers for Paul. They helped keep him safe when people wanted to hurt him. They helped Paul tell others about Christ's love. They served God together.

Doing something kind for someone is a great way to be a good example of Jesus and His love.

Questions

Q How can you work together with your friends to serve Christ?

Q How can you work together with your friends to serve others and show them the love of Jesus? (You and your friend could invite others to church. You could visit your friend if he is sick.)

Q Who are you thankful for? Why?

Activities

✘ Invite a missionary or someone from the community to speak to the children about the work he does and the people who help him do this special work.

✘ Visit a nursing home or an assisted-living center with gifts the children have made or pictures they have drawn.

✘ Help the children make "Jesus Loves You" cards. Have each child pick a special person to receive her card.

Our Friend Jesus

That our Savior, the Son of God, should not only redeem us, but also choose to call us His friends is amazing. The same Jesus who forbade the disciples from keeping the little children from coming to Him still wants us to bring children to Him today. No greater responsibility is given to those who work with children than that of introducing each child to Jesus and helping to nurture that most precious of all relationships. The activities in this section are designed to help you enrich this relationship between the children in your care and their Savior. While these activities are included in this unit on friendship, they may be used at any time throughout the year.

Jesus' Friends Obey Him

"You are My friends if you do what I command. I no longer call you servants, because a servant does not know his master's business. Instead, I have called you friends, for everything that I learned from My Father I have made known to you" (John 15:14–15).

Say: **Jesus calls us "friend." He loves us and helps us show His love to others. When we serve and help others, we show that we are thankful that Jesus calls us friends. We can find out what Jesus wants us to do by reading His words in the Bible, by going to church and studying the Bible with others, and by praying and listening with our hearts.**

Jesus' Friends Love God

Jesus tells us in Matthew 22:37–38:

"Love the Lord your God with all your heart and with all your soul and with all your mind. This is the first and greatest commandment."

How do we show God we love Him?

1. Sing songs of love to Him.

Sing and make music in your heart to the Lord (Ephesians 5:19).

- ✔ "My Jesus, I Love Thee"
- ✔ "Oh, How I Love Jesus"
- ✔ "God Is So Good" (be sure to include the verse "I love Him so.")
- ✔ "More Love to Thee"

2. Go to church to worship Him and to Sunday school to learn more about Him.

"Yet a time is coming and has now come when the true worshipers will worship the Father in spirit and truth, for they are the kind of worshipers the Father seeks. God is spirit, and His worshipers must worship in spirit and in truth" (John 4:23–24).

- ✔ Set up a worship center in your classroom. Include a table with a children's Bible, a cross, and a special cloth.
- ✔ Teach children to handle the Bible with respect and care.
- ✔ Help children memorize verses. Here are some suggestions for doing so:
  - * Say the whole verse with the reference at the end.
  - * Say a few words at a time allowing the children to repeat them phrase by phrase.
  - * Let the children fill in the blank with one word, then two, until the verse is memorized.
  - * Practice saying the verse together and then let the children say the verse alone.

3. Give offerings to help those in need and those spreading the Good News.

Each man should give what he has decided in his heart to give, not reluctantly or under compulsion, for God loves a cheerful giver (2 Corinthians 9:7).

- ✔ Have an offering bank in the classroom.
- ✔ Hold toy, food, and clothing drives for children in need.
- ✔ Collect Bibles for missionaries to use in spreading God's Word.

Jesus' Friends Love Each Other

Jesus also gave us two other ways to show His love. In Matthew 22:39:
"And the second [commandment] is like it: 'Love your neighbor as yourself.'"

And again in John 13:34:
*"A new command I give you: Love one another.
As I have loved you, so you must love one another."*

How do we love our neighbors like we love ourselves?

1. We do things they like to do.
2. We help them when we are able.
3. We listen to what they have to say.

My dear brothers, take note of this: Everyone should be quick to listen, slow to speak and slow to become angry (James 1:19).

✔ Play "Spreading the Good News" with the children to demonstrate how important it is to listen carefully to what others say. Have the children all sit in a circle. Start by whispering one phrase (such as "Jesus loves you!") to the child closest to you. Have that child whisper it to his neighbor until every child has had a chance to whisper it. Have the last person repeat what she heard. See if what she heard is what you said to begin with. Be sure to talk about how important it is to listen to what others say.

We forgive them when they hurt us.
"For if you forgive men when they sin against you, your heavenly Father will also forgive you. But if you do not forgive men their sins, your Father will not forgive your sins" (Matthew 6:14–15).

Say: **God sent His Son, Jesus, to die on the cross for the forgiveness of our sins. Because of Jesus, all of our sins are forgiven. We are sorry for the wrong things we do, and Jesus helps us to do what God wants us to do. Jesus also helps us to forgive others when they do something to hurt us. When we forgive someone else, that means we don't try to hurt that person even if that person has hurt you. It means that we will not be hurtful with our own words and actions.**

Forgiveness Object Lesson

You Will Need:

A large clear bowl filled about ⅔ full with water
Food coloring
Eye dropper
Spoon
Bleach (for adult use only)

How to Do:

1. Set the bowl where the children can see it but from a safe distance. Say: **When we do things that hurt others and hurt God, it is called sin. When we sin it's like making a big ugly stain.**

2. Drip drops of food coloring into the water as you name sins that small children are likely to understand. Say: **When we hit someone because we are angry; when we use words that hurt people and make them sad; when we don't help people when we are able; when we break things on purpose because we're angry; or want to hurt someone, it is like making an ugly stain that won't go away.**

3. Stir the water. Say: **We can't get the stain out by ourselves. We can't make things all right.**

4. Say: **But God forgives us.** Pour bleach into the bowl. Say: **Because Jesus died on the cross and came to life again for us, God forgives our sins. His forgiveness takes away the ugly stains of our sins.**

5. Stir the bleach. (The water will become white.) Say: **God's forgiveness takes away the stains but it doesn't mean everything is just the same as it was before. If we have said hurtful words to someone else, they will still feel hurt. If we have broken something because we were angry, it will have to be either repaired or thrown away. Sin means some things will be damaged or hurt.**

   But God's forgiveness means that even though He doesn't love the sin, He still loves us. And He helps us do for others what He does for us. He helps us forgive others, even when they do things that make us feel sad or angry inside.

Forgiveness Gifts to God

You Will Need:

Tissue or small (jewelry-size) box, one per child
Ribbon long enough to tie around the box, one length per child
A box or basket large enough to hold all the boxes
Treats (snacks, stickers, or any other small gifts)

How to Do:

1. Explain that when someone does something to hurt us we can hold onto that hurt just like we can hold onto this box. That can make us feel hurt or angry. Sometimes we even choose to hold onto our hurt or angry feelings for a long time.
2. But if we are busy holding on to anger or hurt feelings, we can't hold on to the good gifts God wants to share with us. God wants to give us the gifts of His love and grace: blessings, love, and many good things in our lives. But we can't accept these blessings if we are holding onto the anger or hurt.
3. But then we can remember the gift of God's forgiveness. Because He forgives us, we can forgive others. When we forgive someone for Jesus' sake, it's like tying a ribbon around the hurt and turning it into the gift of forgiveness. (Tie ribbons around each child's tissue or box.)
4. Have the children place the "gifts of forgiveness" into the larger basket or box.
5. As each child places his or her gift into the box, place a treat into her hands.
6. Now our hands are free to accept the many gifts God gives us each day.

Jesus' Friends Help Others

I have set you an example that you should do as I have done for you. I tell you the truth, no servant is greater than his master, nor is a messenger greater than the one who sent him (John 13:15–16).

Say: **Jesus is the Son of God. But He didn't tell people to treat Him like a king and to do all kinds of things for Him while He just sat and waited for them to serve Him. He came to serve, not to be served. He served others by teaching them about God and His love, by feeding them when they were hungry, by healing them when they were sick, by forgiving them when they had sinned, and by taking their sins to the cross.**

Jesus tells us to look for ways to help the people around us. Serving others is a way to share the love of Jesus with them. And the love of Jesus is so wonderful— too wonderful to keep to ourselves.

Look for opportunities to involve little ones in helping others in your families, churches, and community.

- ✔ Hold food and clothing drives.
- ✔ Pick up litter.
- ✔ Bring practical gifts or handmade artwork to nursing home and hospital residents.
- ✔ Ask the parents to give the children a special task for helping at home: setting napkins at the table, folding towels, picking up toys, or perhaps feeding a pet.

Jesus' Friends Tell Others about Him

"Therefore go and make disciples of all nations, baptizing them in the name of the Father and of the Son and of the Holy Spirit, and teaching them to obey everything I have commanded you. And surely I am with you always, to the very end of the age" (Matthew 28:19–20).

1. Invite guests to the classroom to hear the children sing songs of praise and worship. Let the children plan, prepare, and serve refreshments to their guests.
2. Invite a missionary to speak to your class about the work he does.
3. Take a collection for a missionary outreach program.

Faith Foundations

Scripture

Read the book *Zacchaeus* (CPH, Arch Book) or tell the story as found in Luke 19:1–9.

Say: **Zacchaeus was very short. He was a little man. He really wanted to see Jesus, but everyone was in his way. So Zacchaeus climbed up into a sycamore tree. (Let's pretend we are climbing up in a tree, so we can see.)**

The people who lived in Zacchaeus's town did not like him very much because he took money from them. When Jesus told Zacchaeus that He wanted to visit his home, the people were very surprised because of the bad things Zacchaeus had done.

But Jesus wanted to teach Zacchaeus about being kind and loving others. Jesus forgave Zacchaeus for doing wrong and He helped Zacchaeus change. Now he wanted Zacchaeus to start doing things right.

Questions

Q Do you like to ask friends to come over to your house? Why?

Q What are your favorite things to do when your friends visit?

Q How do you make your friends feel welcome in your home? Do you share your toys?

Activities

✗ Make a Sycamore Tree

You Will Need:

Small brown paper bags (1 per child)
Green tissue paper
White glue
Colored construction paper

How to Do:

1. Twist a small brown bag to form the tree trunk.
2. Once the tree trunk is formed, tear pieces down from the top of the bag to form the branches.
3. Glue the tree to a piece of construction paper.
4. Tear pieces of the green tissue paper to form the leaves of the tree.
5. Say: **When you look at your tree, think about how Jesus changed Zacchaeus's life and how He loves you.**

   • Ask: **If you have ever been unkind to someone, how can you help that person feel better?** (After some suggestions by the children, you might need to add that they could try drawing a picture for this person explaining that they are sorry.)

✗ Think of ways to make a sad friend smile:

* Take him a new book or coloring book.
* Draw her a happy picture.
* Share a silly story.
* Invite him to play with you.
* Share a toy with her.
* Play a game he likes to play.
* Tell her "Jesus loves you."